Motoring Wit

summersdale

MOTORING WIT

Summersdale Publishers Ltd
46 West Street
Chichester
West Sussex
PO19 1RP
UK

www.summersdale.com

Printed and bound in Great Britain

ISBN: 978-1-84024-703-9

Disclaimer
Every effort has been made to attribute the quotations in
this collection to the correct source. Should there be any
omissions or errors in this respect we apologise and shall
be pleased to make the appropriate acknowledgements in
any future editions.

Motoring Wit

Quips and Quotes for the Auto-Obsessed

Aubrey Malone

Contents

Editor's Note

We all need to get from A to B, but some love to get there more speedily than others. And that's where the love of a good car comes in – though some might argue two wheels are better than four.

Life in the fast lane has many devotees, whether it's speeding down a country road with the top down or watching the professionals vroom around the track at Silverstone. Along with words of inspiration on the joy of motoring from such petrol-heads as Stirling Moss and Paul Newman are some road-rageous comic lines from the best commentators to entertain and delight.

Automobiles all come with frustrations too, whether it's parking the vehicle, paying for it or keeping the police officers happy when they ask 'Who do you think you are – Lewis Hamilton?' *Motoring Wit* also pulls together a gas-guzzling collection of goofy graffiti, idiotic insurance claims and barmy bumper stickers to keep you giggling through the worst rush-hour gridlock.

Fasten your seat belt and fall about laughing at the worst of the driveway models. Henry Ford has a lot to answer for.

THE MEANING
OF MOTORING

If God wanted us to
walk, he'd have given
us pogo sticks instead
of feet. Feet are made
to fit car pedals.

Stirling Moss

No other man-made
device since the
shields and lances of
the ancient knights
fulfils a man's ego
like an automobile.

Sir William Rootes

The wheel was man's greatest invention until he sat behind it.

Sid Caesar

You have your own company, your own temperature control, your own music.

Steven Norris on why cars are better than public transport

The car has become an article of
dress without which we would feel
uncertain, unclad, and incomplete.

Marshall McLuhan

A car is just a giant moving handbag.

Cynthia Heimel

A gas-guzzling
horse on wheels...
exhilaration for the
restless and sudden
death for the unwary.

Rick Bayan's definition of the automobile

MOTOR GRAFFITI

A girl should hang onto her youth – but not while he's driving.

Fjords are the best Swedish cars.

———

An L driver is a Rhodes scholar.

———

People who drink before
they drive are putting the
quart before the hearse.

It takes a lot of bread to own a Rolls.

—•—

Used cars aren't all they're
jacked up to be.

—•—

Buy a Honda if you
have a yen for one.

Hertz Van Rental
was a Dutch painter.

Save petrol. Make roads shorter.

French cars Renault of petrol.

They don't make cars like they auto.

A WINNING FORMULA

There's no secret
to success in motor
racing. You just press
the accelerator to the
floor and steer left.

Bill Vukovich

Formula One is a vast and private Scalextric set for megalomaniac millionaires.

Paul Weaver

Eddie Irvine is brash and abrasive. He's the Ian Paisley of Formula One.

Damon Hill

In my sport the quick are too often listed among the dead.

Jackie Stewart

A dozen daredevils going around in circles, and thousands of cheering spectators waiting for a crack-up.

Rick Bayan on the essence of motor racing

I always felt I would retire when I stopped enjoying racing but it occurred to me recently that I may have to find another reason because I may never stop enjoying it.

Graham Hill

Money is how we keep score
in motor racing nowadays.

Colin Chapman

—•—

I really want to win a race this
year. If I don't, all the guys will
start calling me Tim Henman.

Mark Webber

—•—

I've always tended to the view that...
the whole business is more or less
a waste of good champagne.

Martin Kelmer on Formula One

Nicky Lauda is a single-minded chap. If he found you lying on the ground he would sooner walk over you than around you.

James Hunt

On the day of a big motor race a lot of people want you to sign something just before you get into your car – just so they can say they got your last autograph.

A. J. Foyt

Apprentice racing
drivers think their
mirrors are just
for shaving.

Jody Scheckter

When the flag drops,
the bullshit stops.

Frank Gardner

Motor racing is less of a sport
these days than a commercial
break doing 150 mph.

Peter Dunn

You'll see more overtaking at
your local zebra crossing.

Paul Weaver on the 2005 British Grand Prix

STIRLING WORDS

One cannot really
enjoy speed to the
absolute limit if there's
a destination involved.

Stirling Moss

It's taken me 33 years and a bang
on the head to get my values right.

Stirling Moss

———— ·•· ————

Jackie Stewart was the first of
the modern-style drivers, a man
who drove fast enough to win, but
at the lowest possible speed.

Stirling Moss

There are two things no
man will admit he cannot do
well: drive and make love.

Stirling Moss

It's necessary to relax your
muscles when you race, but it's
fatal to relax your brain.

Stirling Moss

ETERNAL MYSTERIES

Why do short cuts
inevitably make
journeys longer?

Dudley Moore

If it's freight sent by ship it's a cargo, and if it's freight sent by car then it's a shipment!

Dave Allen on the perversity of the language
we use for transporting things

There are ways out of everything apart from the city of Oxford's one-way system.

Simon Mayo

Why is it that anyone going slower
than you in a car is an idiot, and
anyone going faster a maniac?

George Carlin

I saw this car with a 'Baby
on Board' sticker... why
don't they use a cushion?

Steven Wright

I keep everything in the glove compartment of my car except gloves.

Bob Monkhouse

———

There's an unseen force which lets birds know when you've just washed your car.

Denis Norden

———

Ask someone the way, [and] he invariably turns out to be either deaf, senile or a stranger.

Lambert Jeffries

Why is it when a car is causing an obstruction they bloody clamp it?

Dave Allen

Why do they call it rush hour when nothing moves?

Robin Williams

SORRY, OFFICER...

I've just had it serviced
and was checking
to see if the fault
was corrected.

I couldn't see the sign because of that bloody great furniture van.

———•———

I thought you were after someone else so I speeded up to make room for you to get by.

———•———

I had no idea I was going that fast. Thank you for stopping me and letting me know.

I'm afraid the radio was blaring
and I couldn't hear your siren.

I'm just on my way to the
MOT. From what you say,
things don't look too good.

I was just about to reverse.
You don't need your belt
on to do that, do you?

MODEL BEHAVIOUR

What's the difference
between a Ford
and a golf ball?
You can drive a golf
ball 200 yards.

Jackie Mason

A Range Rover is like a
country cottage on wheels.

Jonathan Glancey

My father told me that if I saw a
man in a Rolls Royce you could
be sure he wasn't a gentleman
unless he was a chauffeur.

Earl of Arran

Q: How do you
use the airbags
on a Lada?
A: If you're in
an accident,
start blowing.

Anonymous

The VW Beetle has such a
completely pathetic heater that
on cold days you'd be better
off setting fire to your hair.

Richard Porter

If you stay in Beverley Hills too
long you become a Mercedes.

Dustin Hoffman

Women are like cars. We all
want a Ferrari but we end
up with a station wagon.

Tim Allen

Like a Volvo, Björn Borg is
rugged, has good after-sales
service and is very dull.

Clive James

One enjoys the cheek of a car
company that can take a panelled
sitting room, propel it down the road
at over 100 mph and make as little
noise as a skilled fly-fisherman.

John Whiston on the Rolls Royce

The Model T Ford can be sold
in any colour as long as it's black.

Henry Ford

The E-Type Jag was the
great British phallic symbol.

Christy Campbell

People don't want a cheaper
car. They want an expensive
car that costs less.

Jackie Mason

IDIOTIC
INSURANCE CLAIMS

The pedestrian had
no idea which way to
run, so I ran over him.

The indirect cause of the accident was a little guy in a small car with a big mouth.

———•———

I was thrown from the car as it left the road. I was later found in a ditch by some stray cows.

———•———

To avoid hitting the bumper of the car in front I struck the pedestrian.

I saw a slow-moving, sad-faced old gentleman, as he bounced off the roof of my car.

My car was legally parked as it
backed into the other vehicle.

An invisible car came out of
nowhere, struck my car and vanished.

Windscreen broken. Cause
unknown. Probably voodoo.

The car in front hit the pedestrian
but he got up so I hit him again.

———•———

I had been driving for 40 years
when I fell asleep at the wheel
and had an accident.

———•———

I collided with a stationary
truck coming the other way.

A truck backed through my
windshield into my wife's face.

— · —

A pedestrian hit me and
went under my car.

— · —

The other car collided
with mine without giving
warning of its intention.

In an attempt to kill a fly, I drove into a telephone pole.

I started to turn and it was at this point I noticed a camel and an elephant tethered at the verge. This distraction caused me to lose concentration and hit a bollard.

I was on my way to the doctor with rear end trouble when my universal joint gave way causing me to have an accident.

I started to slow down but the traffic
was more stationary than I thought.

I didn't think the speed limit
applied after midnight.

Q: Could either driver have done
anything to avoid the accident?
A: Travelled by bus?

I was going at about 70 or 80
mph when my girlfriend on the
pillion reached over and grabbed
my testicle so I lost control.

———•———

Coming home, I drove into
the wrong house and collided
with a tree I don't have.

———•———

I pulled into a lay-by with
smoke coming from under the
bonnet. I realised the car was
on fire so took my dog out and
smothered it with a blanket.

I thought my window was down, but I found out it wasn't when I put my head through it.

MEN AND WOMEN

Men are superior
to women. For one
thing, they can urinate
from a speeding car.

Will Durst

A man is at his most useful
when changing a flat tyre.

Rita Rudner

Stick to the same model.

Henry Ford's advice on the formula
for a successful marriage

If it's got tyres or testicles, you're
going to have problems with it.

Roseanne Barr

My licence plate
says PMS.

Wendy Liebman

A woman's age is like [a] car
clock... you know it's set back,
but you're not sure how much.

Tom O'Connor

Men like cars, women like clothes.
Women only like cars because
they take them to clothes.

Rita Rudner

A woman asked her husband,
'Be an angel and let me drive'.
So he did. And he is.

Bob Goddard

Children in the back seat of cars
cause accidents. And accidents in
the back seats of cars cause children.

Sid Caesar

There is no more irresistible
mating call than the imperious
horn at the kerb.

Bergen Evans

When I was a young man, the only
motor vehicle emissions that took
place were while people were having
a naughty in the back seat of one.

Gough Whitlam

The father is concerned with parking
space, the children with outer space
and the mother with closet space.

Evan Esar

I'm the first queen who's
been able to drive.

Queen Elizabeth II

Take up car maintenance and find the class is full of thirty-something women like me, looking for a fella.

Marian Keyes

Men who buy a new car every year usually have trouble committing to a relationship.

Rita Rudner

THE LOVE OF A
GOOD CAR

When a man opens
the car door for his
wife, it's either a new
car or a new wife.

Prince Philip

What Englishman will give his
mind to politics as long as he can
afford to keep a motor car?

George Bernard Shaw

A guy knows he's in love
when he loses interest in
his car for a few days.

Tim Allen

A new addition has been added
to the Dean family. I have
been sleeping with my MG.

James Dean in a letter to his girlfriend

When our cars stop we ring the AA
as soon as we have finished crying.

Joe Bennett

When a man buys a motor
car, he doesn't know what
he's letting himself in for.

Jaroslav Hašek

I'm getting old.
When I squeeze
into a tight parking
space I'm sexually
satisfied for the day.

Rodney Dangerfield

THE LONG ARM
OF THE LAW

I always get out of speeding fines. The cop ends up giving me his business card and saying, 'Let's go out to dinner.'

Paris Hilton, before being sent to prison for driving offences

He said, 'Didn't you see the sign?'
I said, 'Sure, but I don't
believe everything I read.'

Steven Wright on being pulled over by
a cop for ignoring a stop sign

I was stopped for going 53 in a 35-
miles zone. I told 'em I had dyslexia.

George 'Spanky' McFarland

A lady was stopped by a motorcycle cop. She said to him bitterly, 'If I was speeding, so were you!'

Hal Roach

He had his driving licence taken away for life in Ireland. They couldn't overlook the fact that he had managed to drive his car into a corporation bus. Twice.

Elizabeth Harris on her first husband, Richard Harris

I asked the policeman why he
wanted me to blow into the bag.
'My chips are hot,' he said.

Roy 'Chubby' Brown

I was driving so fast because
I was trying to get home
before the petrol ran out.

Dusty Young

I'm so vain I even smile
at speed cameras.

Katy French

BAD DRIVERS

His absent-mindedness
made him a very
dangerous driver... he
was known to change
gears with my kneecap.

Peter Ustinov

Oddly enough, all the bad
drivers I've known died
peacefully in their beds.

Paul Johnson

Most cars have one part that
desperately needs to be replaced:
the nut behind the wheel.

Hal Roach

Taxi drivers are simply not to
be trusted, usually because of
a pronounced death wish.

Robert Morley

It's funny how a wife can spot
a blonde hair at 20 yards and
yet miss the garage doors.

Rodney Dangerfield

Some people drive as if they were anxious to have their accident as quickly as possible to get it over with.

Herbert Prochnow

Ι'm the worst driver... Ι should drive a hearse and cut out the middleman.

Wendy Liebman

I like to drive with my knees. Otherwise how can I put on lipstick and talk on the phone?

Sharon Stone

I picked up a hitch-hiker once.
Well you gotta when you hit 'em.

Emo Philips

—◆—

If you don't like the way I
drive, stay off the sidewalk!

Joan Rivers

—◆—

The freeway is where drivers
under 25 do over 90, and
drivers over 90 do 25.

George Coote

Hand signals are very important
for driving. I usually find that
two fingers work the best.

Roy 'Chubby' Brown

❦

Never lend your car to anyone
to whom you've given birth.

Erma Bombeck

AT THE GARAGE

I said to a garage man, 'Will you service my car?' He looked at it and said, 'Try Lourdes.'

Les Dawson

'If I was you, sir,' he said, 'I'd keep
the oil and change the car.'

George Coote quoting a garage mechanic

Wanted: Man to test motor
batteries, and to take charge.

Sign in a garage window

If you ask me to fix a car it's like
asking Ray Charles to drive it.

Robert Murray

The car gets a flat tyre. Out
of sheer boredom, I imagine,
as it gets driven so seldom.

Alan Bennett

A garage told me my battery
was flat. Big deal. What shape
is it supposed to be?

Fred Allen

A grimy surgeon who... rarely
loses a patient, although he
sometimes performs unnecessary
organ transplants.

Rick Bayan defining a garage mechanic

My dad used to spend ages
tinkering under the bonnet of his
Capri. Then it would invariably
have to be towed to a garage to
repair the damage he'd caused.

Robert Greenway

CROSSING BORDERS

The first
commandment of life
in Ireland... Thou
shalt never, under
any circumstances,
wash a car.

Rowan Atkinson

Those who think the war in Beirut is dangerous haven't seen the traffic.

P. J. O'Rourke

The Italians should never, ever have been let in on the invention of the motor car.

Bill Bryson

I once saw a road sign in Ireland that said, 'Warning: this is a one-way cul-de-sac' at both ends.

Spike Milligan

To a Miami driver,
a green light means
'Proceed', a yellow
one 'Proceed
much faster' and a
red one 'Proceed
while gesturing'.

Dave Barry

What was the most hazardous
part of my expedition to Africa?
Crossing Piccadilly Circus.

J. M. Barrie

Ireland's roundabouts are a
kind of vehicular Pamplona.

David Monaghan

What would be a road hazard
anywhere else, in the Third
World is probably the road.

P. J. O'Rourke

In Milan, traffic lights are instructions. In Rome they're suggestions. But in Naples they're Christmas decorations.

Antonio Martino

In Naples

A tourist is someone who goes 3,000 miles to get a picture of himself in front of his car.

Herbert Prochnow

When you ask
someone for
directions in Ireland
you get a story,
not directions.

Louis Marcus

Never ask an English person for directions. They're too polite to tell you if they don't know the way.

Joe O'Connor

The speed of travel these days is amazing... you can be at Heathrow just 3 ½ hours after leaving central London.

Fred Metcalf

GRIDLOCK

The traffic jams
in Gower are so
famous, people arrive
in hundreds in their
cars just to see them.

Gren Jones

Traffic is so bad in London today, the only way to get across Trafalgar Square is to be born there.

Frank Campbell

The car was moving so slowly on the M25 I had to leave it twice to make payments on it.

Edward Phillips

As you get older you need to sleep more. My favourite time is on the motorway, during rush hour.

Bob Hope

I went down to campaign
against the bypass scheme
but I got stuck in traffic.

Harry Hill

***

Put all the lights on red and
keep them that way.

George Kaufman on how to solve the
New York City traffic problem

***

The city is turning into the
largest car park in Europe.

Brendan O'Carroll on Dublin's gridlock problem

KEEP ON TRUCKING

I wonder what
language truck
drivers are using
now that everyone
else is using theirs?

Beryl Pfizer

Perhaps the thing I might do best is
to be a long-distance lorry driver.

Princess Anne

You never realise how many
parts a car has until it hits
the end of a big truck.

Don Rickles

If an Englishman
gets run down by a
truck, he apologises
to the truck.

Jackie Mason

We were making love in the back of
a truck and we got carried away.

Spike Milligan

A lorry carrying onions has
been overturned on the M1.
Motorists are asked to find
a hard shoulder to cry on.

Gyles Brandreth

OLD BANGERS

I saw a second-hand
car last week that
was so old it had
bifocal headlights.

Edward Philips

It had a heated windscreen at the back to keep your hands warm while you're pushing it.

Hal Roach

The best time to buy a used car is when it's new.

Dan Whitney

Very few cars enjoy even
moderately good health, and
driving one is like nursing an
invalid who only very occasionally
rallies from a fatal illness.

Robert Morley

———

I call my car Flattery because
it gets me nowhere.

Henny Youngman

If all the stations are rock 'n' roll, there's a good chance the transmission is shot.

Larry Lujack's advice on buying a used car – punch the buttons on the radio

The only part of the car that didn't make a noise when in motion was the hooter.

Denis Norden

Would you buy a used
car from this man?

Anti-Richard Nixon poster from 1968

'Many optional extras' on a
car ad means 'Has wheels,
battery and heater.'

Russell Ash

Motor cars have never been
quite the same for me since
people stopped winding
them up at the front.

Arthur Marshall

It's difficult not to feel
sorry for derelict cars.

Virginia Graham

Middle age is when you're more worried about how long your car will last instead of how fast it'll go.

Eddie Irvine

PARKING FINE

Advice on Love,
Marriage and Parking.

Sign outside fortune-teller's booth

Dying is easy. Parking is difficult.

Walter Matthau

❦

I would kill muggers, rapists and child killers for a start, and then people who parked illegally.

Michael Winner on what he would put right if he were God

His wife is the only person in the world who parks her car by ear.

Peter Cagney

———— ⦁ ————

Parking is such street sorrow.

Herb Caen

———— ⦁ ————

Robinson's Law: the guy you beat out of a prime parking space is the one you have to see for a job interview.

Cal Robinson

Parking space: an unoccupied place
on the other side of the street.

Pete Hagan

———•———

Thunder is God trying
to parallel park.

Graham Norton

———•———

I used to complain that I had no
shoes until I met a man with no
feet. Then I complained because
he got the good parking spot.

Jim Evarts

To my wife, double
parking means on
top of another car.

Dave Barry

Pay your parking tickets,
Mr Coulthard.

**Prince Rainier after Coulthard won the
Monaco Grand Prix in 2000.**

Someone complimented me
on my driving today. They left
a little note on the windscreen
saying 'Parking fine.'

Tommy Cooper

There are people working
in McDonald's in Soho
who can see parking meters
earning more than they are.

Simon Evans

I don't have a problem with San
Francisco parking. I drive a forklift.

Jim Samuels

Give a woman an inch
and she'll park on it.

Chief Constable of Gloucester

⬥

Sidney Lumet is one of the fastest
directors I've ever worked with.
He could double park in front of a
whorehouse and still not get a ticket.

Paul Newman

TWO WHEELS BETTER THAN FOUR?

I'm not a daredevil.
I'm an explorer.

Evel Knievel

A casualty surgeon in Manhattan tells me he and his colleagues had a one-word nickname for bikers: Donors.

Stephen Fry

Riding a moped is like being on a hairdryer. Dogs are walking faster than you're going.

Eddie Izzard

There's no retirement plan for motocrossers.

Thomas McGuane

You'd be amazed at how
many teenagers get a car by
asking for a motorcycle.

**James Varley on learning the art of
negotiation at an early age**

Definition of a sadistic
birthday gift: a down payment
on a Harley Davidson.

Sam Levenson

Motorcyclists who don't wear
helmets should have their heads
examined... and they usually do.

Fred Metcalf

I've just married
a machine.

James Dean after buying his first motorcycle

Why not give your son a
motorcycle for his last birthday?

Colin Bowles

⬥

Those for whom automobiles
provide insufficient risk
to life and limb.

Rick Bayan on motorcyclists

These days I prefer
motorcycles to sex.

Mickey Rourke

And then there was the
intellectually challenged Evel
Knievel imitator who tried to drive
over thirty motorbikes in a bus.

Anonymous

ACCIDENTS HAPPEN

It's the overtakers
who keep the
undertakers busy.

William Ewart Pitts

After you've heard two eyewitness
accounts of an auto accident, it
makes you wonder about history.

Herbert Prochnow

———— • ————

A man is knocked down by
a car every three hours. He
must be getting fed up of it.

Shaun Connors

———— • ————

I'm insured with Mafia plc. Its policy
is simple: You hit us, we hit you.

Joe Greenwood

I was sure it was my mother-in-law's car that had knocked me down. I'd recognise that laugh anywhere.

Henny Youngman

Most accidents occur within five minutes of the home. Move house.

Milton Berle

The 'Act of God' designation...
means, roughly, that you cannot
be insured for the accidents that
are most likely to happen.

Alan Coren on insurance policies

I told her that if she has an accident
the newspapers will print her age.

Jan Murray's idea for making his
wife drive more carefully

They asked me to become a
Jehovah's Witness but I refused. I
didn't even see the bloody accident.

Paul Malone

I'm so unlucky I run into accidents
started by other people.

Rodney Dangerfield

Avoid accidents on the road:
drive on the footpath.

Bob Monkhouse

If I have an accident I just call
the insurance company and they
tell me it wasn't their fault.

Fred Metcalf on the definition of no-fault car insurance

My wife called me and said there
was water in the carburettor. I said
'Where is it?' 'In the lake,' she replied.

Henny Youngman

SAFETY FIRST

He's so nervous he
even wears a seat belt
during a drive-in movie.

Neil Simon

I'm a very careful driver. I always look both ways before hitting something.

Fred Metcalf

Please drive carefully. The life you save may owe me money.

Les Dawson

The best car safety
device is a rear-view
mirror with a cop in it.

Dudley Moore

Horsepower was much safer
when only horses had it.

Herbert Prochnow

I do not participate in any sport with
ambulances at the bottom of the hill.

Erma Bombeck

THINK BEFORE
YOU DRINK

One for the road
could be the pint
of no return.

Celia Haddon

Don't drink and drive. Leave
it on the dashboard.

Brendan Grace

———•———

I gave my car away to a good
charity, Alcoholics Anonymous.

Wayne Riley

———•———

The driver is safe when the
roads are dry and the roads are
safe when the driver is dry.

Conor Faughnan

I've decided to stop driving
drunk. I can never remember
where I parked the bloody car.

Dave Allen

There's a new association now
called the AAAA. They'll
tow you home if you're too
drunk to make it on your own.

Paul Lynam

If you drink, don't
drive. Don't even putt.

Dean Martin

People who are driven to drink rarely
have trouble finding a parking spot.

Herbert Prochnow

Policemen are wrong when they
say alcohol and petrol don't mix.
They do. But it tastes horrible.

Jim Davidson

DITCHING THE WHEELS

A pedestrian ought to be legally allowed to toss at least one hand grenade at a motorist every day.

Brendan Francis

Never take lifts from
strange men. And
all men are strange.

Mary Mannion

The best advice for pedestrians today is to buy a suit of armour.

Herbert Prochnow

Pedestrians rely on food for fuel and need no special parking facilities.

Lewis Mumford

A pedestrian is a man who has two cars – one being driven by his wife and the other by one of his children.

Robert Bradbury

Walking while sober these
days is almost as dangerous
as driving while drunk.

Simon Halston

Have a drive in one of our cars
and you'll never walk again.

Sign in a garage

There are only two types of
pedestrians: the quick and the dead.

Thomas Dewar

LIFE IN THE FAST LANE

Nigel Mansell should have 'Who dares whines' embroidered on his overalls.

Simon Barnes

I like to win. I despise that in
myself but it's all there is.

Paul Newman

———◆———

The first thing that I ever
found I had any grace in.

Paul Newman on motor sports

———◆———

At my age, to win and have a pulse
on the same day is pretty good.

Paul Newman at 68

In my day, racing was 75 per cent car and 25 per cent driver. Today it's 95 per cent car. Skill hardly counts any more.

Juan Manuel Fangio

Your profile resembles that of John Barrymore, but then your automobile racing will probably soon take care of that.

Edna Ferber to James Dean

It's impossible to travel faster than
the speed of light, and not desirable.
One's hat keeps blowing off.

Woody Allen

I don't mind having an accident
when I can see it coming.

Nigel Mansell

I'd rather have an accident
than fall in love. That's how
much I love motor racing.

Lella Lombardi

What you've got
to remember about
Michael Schumacher
is that under that
cold professional
Germanic exterior
there beats a
heart of... stone.

Damon Hill

When the car somersaulted at 280 mph as I was going for the record, my only thought was, 'God, the wife is going to kill me for this.'

Barry Bowles on drag racing

❧

Rally points scoring is 20 points for the fastest, 18 for the second fastest and right down to six points for the slowest fastest.

Murray Walker

Nigel Mansell is the only man who goes to Nick Faldo for charisma bypasses.

Nick Hancock

— • —

Here's Giacomelli, driving like the veteran he's not.

Murray Walker

— • —

Racing is the only time I feel whole.

James Dean

STATESIDE

Driving is America's last surviving form of guerrilla warfare.

Gene Perret

Boston's freeway system was clearly designed by a person who had spent his childhood crashing toy trains.

Bill Bryson

In Miami it's considered acceptable to go through a red light as long as you can still remember when it was yellow.

Dave Barry

Everything is drive-through in California. They even have a burial service called Jump-in-the-Box.

Wil Shriner

They drive so crazy in Chicago that anything moving slower than 65 mph is considered a house.

Joe Joshua

An American is a man who has two legs, four wheels and a spare tyre.

Herbert Prochnow

Nobody has ever successfully
travelled across Manhattan
in a motor vehicle.

Dave Barry

One hand on wheel, one hand
on non-fat double decaff
cappuccino, cradling cellphone,
brick on accelerator, gun in lap.

Anonymous joke about Californian drivers

L-PLATES

The driving instructor told me to keep my eyes on the road. That's why I crashed into the telegraph pole.

Ritchie Doherty

I don't know if I've got my driver's test yet. I have to wait till the test instructor gets out of hospital.

Jenny O'Reilly

Not long. Just three trees, two lamp posts and a pedestrian.

Edward Phillips' response when asked how long he had been driving

In golf you never hit anything.

Jim Campbell on the difference between learning
to play golf and learning to drive a car

———◆———

Q: What is the difference between
a flashing red traffic light and a
flashing yellow traffic light?
A: The colour.

Answer to a driving theory question

If your wife wants to learn to drive, don't stand in her way.

Sam Levenson

Q: What changes would occur in your lifestyle if you could no longer drive lawfully?
A: I would be forced to drive unlawfully.

Answer to a driving theory question

WARNING SIGNS

Last petrol station until the next one.

Sign spotted in rural England

Last chance for gas. The next
ten filling stations are mirages!

Garage sign in Las Vegas

When this sign is under water,
the road is impassable.

What else could orange cones mean ~ psychedelic witches embedded in asphalt?

Karin Babbitt on the sign 'Orange cones mean men at work'

Please maintain speed
at 25 mph. P.S. Skodas
– do the best you can.

Mountain road sign

Drivers kindly note – this is
the wrong road to Dublin.
Do not take it.

Notice outside Irish garage

I thought: does it? That
makes a change.

**Tony Hancock on seeing a sign
saying 'Road works ahead'**

ROAD RAGE

There is no class of
person more moved by
hate than the motorist.

C. R. Hewitt

Some motorists almost live in their
motor cars. It gratifies me to state
that these motorists generally
die in their motor cars too.

G. K. Chesterton

All power corrupts, and
horsepower corrupts absolutely.

John Hillaby

Car sickness: the feeling
you get each month when
the payments fall due.

J. B. Morton

Do you remember the days
when it used to cost more to
buy a car than to insure it?

George Burns

Nothing depreciates a car
more than your next door
neighbour driving a new one.

Leopold Fechtner

Until you've learned
to drive you've
never really learned
how to swear.

Robert Paul

Car owners of the world unite.
You have nothing to lose but your
manners, and someone else's life.

Colin MacInnes

Wouldn't it be nice if the
wattage of a car stereo couldn't
exceed the IQ of the driver?

Robert Maine

Get a large road map. It will
tell you all you want to know
– except how to fold it again.

Herbert Prochnow

He had a two-way stereo in
his car: his wife in the front
and her mother in the back.

Bob Monkhouse

There are no liberals
behind steering wheels.

Russell Baker

Like a bunch of sheep the drivers
cluster about the sheepdog with
seat belts fastened, hands on the
wheel at ten to two, mobiles in their
crotches and butter-wouldn't-
melt expressions on their faces.

Boris Johnson on what happens
when drivers spot a police car

WACKY RACES

Except for his car
he's the only man
on the track.

Murray Walker

At last a smile from Jacques
Villeneuve to match his bleached hair.

Jonathan Ledgard

❖

David Coulthard looks like he
borrowed the bottom of his head
from Sophie Ellis-Bextor.

From an article in *The Guardian*

❖

He's completely
unoverawed by Senna.

James Hunt

Mansell is taking it easy. Oh no he isn't – it's a lap record.

Murray Walker

Mansell, Senna, Prost. Put them in any order and you end up with the same three drivers.

Derek Warwick

Greg Strange needs no introduction. He's a motoring correspondent for LBC.

Carol Thatcher

Nigel Mansell is a highly experienced driver with an unblemished record of accidents.

Samantha Cohen, Nigel Mansell's representative, after he had been arrested for speeding

PARK AND RIDE

The only times
I ever knew the
buses of Dublin to
go fast is when I'm
running for them.

Brendan Behan

My mother's idea of economy was
to take a bus ride to the Ritz.

Lady Trumpington

He became a bus driver so he
could tell people where to get off.

Peter Cook

The wife doesn't like to have
her hair blown about.

John Prescott explaining why he drove from his
hotel to the Labour Party Conference in 1999

Dublin's public transport system is called the DART, which stands for Dublin Area Rapid Transport. It's just as well we're not Florence.

Kim Bielenberg

John Prescott's idea of a park and ride scheme is to park one Jaguar and drive away in another.

William Hague

It's too bad that all the people who really know how to run the country are busy driving taxicabs.

George Burns

CAR-AZY

Cars should have silent horns. Then they wouldn't disturb people in the night.

Seamus O'Leary

I say, old son, you're doing very well, but should you be trying to change gear with the handbrake?

Hugh Griffith to Peter O'Toole

I had to stop driving for a while. The tyres got dizzy.

Steven Wright

Did you hear about the man who reversed into a car boot sale and sold his engine?

Frank Carson

Driving hasn't been
the same since I
installed funhouse
rear-view mirrors.

Steven Wright

Whenever I rent a car
I reverse everywhere
to cut down on
the mileage rate.

Woody Allen

Who needs Disney World? My kids get just as much of a thrill when we drive through the car wash.

Oliver Coe

Don't rush. The sooner you fall behind, the more time you have to catch up.

Roy Noble

I used to be afraid of flying until I bought a car.

Bob Monkhouse

BUMPER STICKERS

My karma just ran
over my dogma.

When God made women
drivers he was only joking.

———

Jim could not fix this.

———

Happiness is driving over
a traffic warden's foot.

Please pass quietly, driver asleep.

Drive like hell: you'll get there.

Passion wagon. Don't laugh
– your daughter may be in here.

Preserve wildlife.
Pickle a traffic warden.

Never drive faster than your
guardian angel can fly.

The next time you park this
close, bring a can-opener.

For blondes I accelerate.
For brunettes I slow down.
For redheads I reverse.

———•———

This driver gives two-fingered
hand signals only.

———•———

I own the car. It's the petrol
that's on the HP.

Make love not war ~
see driver for details.

This car has been powered by
Jessica Alba's knicker elastic.

—••—

Watch my rear end, not hers.

—••—

Please tailgate – I need the money.